KFK KINGFISHER KNOWLEDGE

ANIMAL GIANTS

KFK KINGFISHER KNOWLEDGE

ANIMAL GIANTS

Barbara Taylor

Foreword by
Kathryn S. Fuller

KINGFISHER

BOSTON

Editor: Vicky Weber
Coordinating editor: Stephanie Pliakas
Designers: Mark Bristow, Carol Ann Davis
Picture researcher: Rachael Swann
DTP manager: Nicky Studdart
DTP operator: Primrose Burton
Senior production controller: Deborah Otter
Proofreaders and Indexer: Sheila Clewley, Terri McCargar
Consultant: David Burnie
Artwork archivists: Wendy Allison, Jenny Lord

KINGFISHER
a Houghton Mifflin Company imprint
222 Berkeley Street
Boston, Massachusetts 02116
www.houghtonmifflinbooks.com

First published in 2004
10 9 8 7 6 5 4 3 2 1
1SBF/0504/TWP/MA(MA)/130ARM/F

Copyright © Kingfisher Publications Plc 2004

LIBRARY OF CONGRESS CATALOGING-IN-PUBLICATION DATA
Taylor, Barbara, 1954–.
Animal giants/Barbara Taylor—1st ed.
p. cm.—(Kingfisher knowledge)
Contents: Largest on land—Titans of the skies—Giants of the water.
Summary: Provides information on the largest animals of land, air, and sea.
1. Animals—Juvenile literature. [1. Animals.] I. Title. II. Series.
QH49.T29 2004
590—dc22   2003061898

ISBN 0-7534-5770-9

Printed in Singapore

GO FURTHER . . .
INFORMATION PANEL KEY:

- web sites and further reading
- career paths
- places to visit

SCALE BOX

Where possible, we have tried to illustrate the size of the animals in this book by showing them next to another object such as a human or a tree. This has not been achievable in every case, so on some pages there is a small scale box (see right), which gives the sizes of all animals on the page in relation to a 5.7-ft. (1.75-m)-tall human.

giant tortoise   Galápagos hawk

WARNING

Most of the animal giants in this book are extremely dangerous wild predators and should not be approached either in the wild or in a zoo.

NOTE TO READERS

The web site addresses listed in this book are correct at the time of publishing. However, due to the ever-changing nature of the Internet, web site addresses and content can change. Web sites can contain links that are unsuitable for children. The publisher cannot be held responsible for changes in web site addresses or content or for information obtained through third-party web sites. We strongly advise that Internet searches should be supervised by an adult.

ABOUT THIS BOOK

As you read this book remember that there is still a lot we do not know about giant animals and why they grow to such huge sizes. Many of the explanations for their record-breaking statistics are theories—ideas that people, especially scientists, have suggested but have not proved. More scientific research and exciting new discoveries of both fossilized animals and living creatures (which are being made all the time) may change or add to these explanations in the future.

Contents

Foreword

Of all the animals on the planet, the largest seem to intrigue us the most. How do giraffes' long legs and necks help them find food? Can butterflies grow to be larger than some birds? Is it true that some snakes grow as long as 30 feet?

In this book, *Animal Giants*, you will learn about some of nature's super-sized creatures, among the most amazing animals in the world. As you read, try to picture yourself in the places where these creatures live—rain forests, grasslands, the ocean—and imagine how they eat, raise their young, and survive in their habitats. Some of these animal giants have babies that are born larger than the largest adult human being. Some are so big that you could even stand up inside their mouths. And sadly, some of these animal giants are disappearing because they no longer have enough places to live.

When animals lose their habitats, they aren't the only ones affected. These animal giants often play a crucial role in the web of life because they serve as keystone species—species that are essential to keeping the whole environment in which they live healthy. If they disappear, many other species that rely on them in some way will also disappear. For example, as elephants wander they distribute the seeds from trees and other plants they eat. Many plant species must pass through an elephant's digestive tract before they can germinate—as many as one third of tree species in west African forests rely on elephants in this way. So by protecting elephants, we can save many other species that live alongside them.

After you read *Animal Giants* you may find you have a new favorite animal or learn that an animal you care about needs protection. Some may be scary enough that you hope never to meet them in person, while others might have you dreaming about a trip to an exotic location. But whatever you think about these animal giants, consider what you can do to help save them for the future of our planet. Everyone, including you, has a role to play. And groups like my organization, World Wildlife Fund, exist to help you, your family, and your community work together to save these important species.

Kathryn S. Fuller

Kathryn S. Fuller
President and CEO
World Wildlife Fund

ostrich

CHAPTER 1

Largest on land

Any person standing next to one of the huge dinosaurs would barely be able to touch its knees, and its long neck would tower way up in the sky. No land animals today reach such a colossal size—and, in fact, a lot of the biggest animals have been hunted and killed by humans. Nevertheless you may be surprised to learn that there are still elephants, bears, and ostriches that look down on people from great heights, as well as snakes as long as a bus and insects bigger than mice. Sound unbelievable? Sound scary? Keep reading, and meet some of these extreme animals. Prepare to be amazed!

Giants of ancient lands

The biggest and heaviest land animals of all time were the long-necked dinosaurs. The largest were longer than a tennis court and almost three times taller than a giraffe. Their gigantic weight must have made the ground shake as they plodded along. One of the most colossal, *Brachiosaurus*, weighed as much as 15 African elephants! Why did they grow so big? No one can be sure, but scientists have a lot of different ideas.

▲ These three long-necked dinosaurs, *Supersaurus* (left), *Ultrasauros* (center), and *Seismosaurus* (right), may have been the biggest of their kind. No complete skeletons have yet been found, and their exact size and weight are the subject of great debate. The *Ultrasauros* bones discovered so far may even have come partly from a *Brachiosaurus* and partly from a *Supersaurus*.

Too big to attack

You may be surprised to learn that the average dinosaur was as big as an elephant and that some dinosaurs were only the size of chickens! It was the huge bulk of the long-necked plant eaters that has given the dinosaurs their reputation for immensity. Being big definitely had its benefits—it made it easier for the huge herbivores, such as *Brachiosaurus* and *Diplodocus*, to survive attacks by the smaller, meat-eating dinosaurs. The giant survivors passed on their characteristics of large size to their offspring, which helped them survive. Proportions increased, generation after generation, until the size of the long-necked herbivores was eventually limited by the problems of finding enough food to eat and supporting the weight of such a huge body.

Big eaters

The long-necked dinosaurs had plenty of plant food to eat since they could reach leaves high up in the trees, and their long digestive systems could process and digest large quantities of plants, even tough ones. Inside their huge stomachs microscopic bacteria helped the dinosaurs break down their food, generating heat as they did so. A lot of heat in a big stomach would have speeded up the digestion, allowing the animal to grow more quickly.

Slow movers

As they strolled around looking for food the long-necked dinosaurs moved at around the same speed as a person walking quickly. They were much too heavy to run and would probably have broken a lot of bones if they had tried. They walked on four massive, pillarlike legs, which supported their bulk. And bulky they were—some of them weighed more than 80 tons. Their arched backbones reinforced the body like a suspension bridge. However, many of the bones in the skeleton were lightweight—hollow bones in the neck, backbone, and tail reduced the overall weight of the body.

Small beginnings

Female dinosaurs may have been bigger than males to help them withstand the pressures of laying eggs and caring for their young. Yet even the biggest dinosaurs laid relatively small eggs—the largest ones were the size of a small melon. If they had been any bigger, they would have needed thicker shells to stop them from collapsing. Then it would have been difficult for the babies developing inside the eggs to get enough oxygen to keep them alive, and the babies would have found it difficult to hatch.

Ice Age giants

Dinosaurs were not the only giants from ancient lands. During the last Ice Age, which ended around 10,000 years ago, other giant mammals roamed the land. These were beasts such as woolly mammoths, which could grow up to 15 ft. (4.5m) in height, with tusks more than 17 ft. (5.2m) long; giant ground sloths that were almost as big as modern elephants; and giant armadillos the size of small cars. The harsh conditions may have encouraged the development of these giants because super-sized species are better at competing for scarce resources such as food. Being large may also have helped them survive the cold because big animals cool down more slowly than smaller ones. This is because they have a smaller body surface on the outside (compared to their huge volume inside) through which they lose heat.

◄ Long-necked dinosaurs, such as this *Brachiosaurus* (center, right), had relatively small heads, which were large enough to reach for plant food but small enough not to weigh down the long neck. They may have had a powerful heart and special muscles in the neck to pump the blood all the way up to the head, as well as valves to stop blood from flowing backward. Meat eaters, such as *Ceratosaurus* (center, left), had much shorter, stronger necks, with big, powerful heads to savagely bite and hold their prey.

The African elephant

All the really large land animals today are mammals, including the biggest and strongest of all—the African elephant. A large male weighs as much as 80 people! This jumbo animal also has the largest ears and the longest nose of any living creature. It has a large brain in relation to its body size, as humans do. Elephants are very intelligent animals with a remarkable capacity for memory.

Supporting skeleton

An African elephant has an extremely strong, bony skeleton to support its colossal weight. All elephants' legs are straight and are positioned directly underneath the body like the legs of a table. The bones in a male elephant's legs grow until it is 35 to 45 years old. In females this growth stops at around the age of 25. Because males grow during most of their lives, they may end up twice as heavy as females. Big, strong males are more likely to win fights for females.

◄ This charging elephant holds its ears out to the side as a warning—to make itself look bigger and more threatening. If its ears were held flat, with the head down and the trunk folded back out of harm's way, this would show that the elephant intends to finish the charge with an attack. Although elephants usually move slowly, they can suddenly speed up to 25 mph (40km/h)—that is much faster than a person can run!

▼ When it is born, after almost two years inside its mother, a baby elephant weighs up to an astonishing 250 lbs. (113kg). However, it is still small enough to be attacked by lions and hyenas, so it stays close to its mother and the rest of the herd. A calf drinks around 3 gal. (11L) of its mother's nourishing milk every day and puts on weight very fast—at a rate of around 22–44 lbs. (10–20kg) per month. Calves continue to drink their mother's milk until they are four to six years old.

Tusks and teeth

An elephant has only four teeth inside its mouth at any one time. Each tooth is very big, weighing more than a brick! These massive molar teeth have sharp ridges to help the elephant grind up its tough plant food. And they certainly have a job to do—a male may eat as much as 663 lbs. (300kg) of plant material every day. The teeth start growing in at the back of the mouth, move slowly forward, and break up or fall out at the front. New teeth replace the old ones. At around the age of 70 an elephant's last set of teeth wears away. This means it cannot chew its food well, and its life comes to an end.

An African elephant usually has two extra front teeth, called tusks. These are made of ivory and grow outside its mouth throughout its life. The longest tusks measured 11.5 ft. (3.5m), and the heaviest ones weighed 260 lbs. (117kg). Elephants with large tusks are rare today because so many have been shot for their ivory. This valuable material is easy to carve, lasts a long time, and is worth a lot of money.

spongy heel cushion

tips of toes

▲ An elephant rests its enormous weight on the tips of its toes and on its spongy heel cushions, which work like huge shock absorbers. This muffles the sound of objects underfoot, making the elephant a surprisingly silent giant.

Big ears

The size of tablecloths, African elephants' ears are three times the size of Asian elephants' ears, most likely because they live in hotter places. The elephants flap these huge ears like fans to cool themselves down. This is important because their big bodies lose heat slowly, and they cannot sweat to cool down.

African elephant

◀ Standing up to 9.2 ft. (2.8m) tall on its back legs, this Kodiak bear, named Bart, towers over its keeper in a friendly wrestling match. You can see Bart's huge front claws, which are able to grow as long as a human hand. In the wild these claws are deadly weapons but are also very useful when digging up food and making dens in the winter.

Bear facts

Imagine standing in front of a bear that weighs eight times more than you do and can stretch to a height of almost 10 ft. (3m). You aren't likely ever to witness such a sight firsthand since the largest bears—the polar bear and the Kodiak bear—usually prefer to avoid people in the wild. This is lucky because they have fiery tempers and can run faster than Olympic sprinters!

Ferocious force

The largest bear ever to have walked on Earth was also the largest known carnivorous mammal on land. At twice the size of the Kodiak bear, the short-faced bear was truly awe inspiring. It lived millions of years ago in North America and probably hunted ancient camels, bison, and horses. Modern wild bears are smaller than this huge beast, but they are no less fearsome. Polar bears, Kodiak bears, and grizzly bears (a type of brown bear) are the largest meat eaters found on land today. Their size and strong bodies make them completely intimidating predators.

Body-building diet

Polar bears are the only bears that eat only meat; other wild bears will eat almost anything, from roots and leaves to insects and deer. Grizzly bears don't eat much meat, but when they do hunt, they are terrifying. They chase large animals, such as caribou, using their strong shoulders and paws to knock the prey off of its feet. They can crush the skulls of their victims with one blow and can crack open the leg bones with their powerful jaws in order to reach the juicy marrow inside.

Among the brown bears, the champion heavyweights are the Kodiak bears of Kodiak Island in Alaska. They can weigh as much as a small car. Kodiak bears can grow to enormous sizes because they live in a mild, moist climate with abundant food supplies. As well as having plenty of berries and plants to eat, Kodiak bears also feast on salmon, which is rich in fat and body-building protein.

Unique giant

Despite being called "giant," the extraordinary and unique giant panda is the second-smallest bear. It is 5.3 ft. (1.6m) tall—around the height of an average adult woman—and weighs up to 276 lbs. (125kg). Many people think that the giant panda is a member of the raccoon family, but genetic tests show that it is closely related to bears, although it does not really behave like them. The giant panda does not hibernate and is a vegetarian, relying on bamboo for up to 99 percent of its food.

▶ On its front paws below the first finger a giant panda has a false thumb, which looks like a tough knob. The panda uses this pad to help it hold on to bamboo stems. The strong, curved claws are used to climb trees and to dig.

▼ A giraffe looks down on the world from the huge height of up to 20 ft. (6m) above the ground—higher than a city bus. The giraffe needs a large heart to pump blood all the way up its neck, which can grow as long as 8 ft. (2.4m). This graceful giant not only has a long neck, but it also has a very long tongue, which can reach around to lick its eyes and ears. It uses this flexible tongue to help it strip leaves from branches that are high up above the ground.

Remarkable body parts

From enormous horns, tusks, and antlers to huge eyes, ears, and noses, some animals have truly remarkable body parts. Often the whole animal is gigantic, but small animals sometimes have extra-large features—for example, a bush baby's huge eyes dominate its tiny face and help it see in the dark. Big body parts can help with all kinds of things such as finding food, winning a mate, avoiding attacks, or staying warm or cool.

Finding food

Extremely long body parts make it easier to find food in places that other animals have no hope of reaching. A giraffe's tall neck and an elephant's long, flexible trunk allow them to reach food that is high up in the trees. The long, sticky tongues of anteaters and woodpeckers allow them to access the narrow places where insects hide and to lap up as many tiny creatures as possible in a short time. The toucan's long bill helps it reach fruit hanging from thin twigs that are too small to land on, while pelicans have large, pouchlike bills to help them catch their fishy food. The Australian pelican has the longest bill of any bird. This amazing feature grows to lengths of 13–18 in. (34–38cm) and can carry more food than can be held in the pelican's stomach.

▼ Giant anteaters usually extend their 23-in. (60-cm)-long tongues into ant and termite nests. The insects stick to the tongue and are pulled back into the anteater's mouth. These unusual creatures can flick their tongues in and out around 150 times per minute and eat an incredible 30,000 insects per day.

Mega headgear

There are three types of huge headgear—horns, tusks, and antlers. All of them are used for defensive purposes and for fighting rivals, while tusks may also be used to gather food. However, each one is made from a different substance, and they grow in a variety of ways. Horns are made from keratin (the same material as human hair and nails); antlers are made from bone; and tusks are extra-long teeth made of a hard material called dentin. Horns and tusks usually last throughout an animal's lifetime, while antlers are shed and regrown each year.

The largest horns, tusks, and antlers grow on the most enormous animals. The longest horns belong to the wild water buffalo—they have a spread as wide as two grown men lying end to end. The horns are hollow, so they are not as heavy as you might think. The world's largest deer, the moose, has the biggest antlers, with a span of up to 6.6 ft. (2m). And the African elephant—the most immense land animal—has the largest tusks. The longest ones ever recorded measured an amazing 11.5 ft. (3.5m)—that is about half the width of the goal on a soccer field.

▼ The gigantic front horn of a white rhinoceros can grow twice as long as a person's arm. Many rhinos have been killed for this valuable headgear, and some species are in danger of extinction. The horns are used to make medicines and dagger handles.

Staying warm or cool

Large body parts may help mammals control their body temperatures. The large ears of elephants, fennec foxes, and jackrabbits act like personal heaters, giving off body heat and cooling down the animals. The musk ox grows the longest hair of any mammal. The hairs on its outer coat can reach around 3 ft. (1m) long and keep it warm in its Arctic habitat.

▶ Opening its jaws for a dental checkup, this hippo shows what "open wide" can really mean! A hippo's lips are around 27 in. (70cm) in width, and the tusks in its lower jaw grow up to 19.5 in. (50cm) long. These tusks are strong enough to make holes in the side of a wooden boat but are only used for defense or fighting rivals.

Island giants

Real, live dragons; tortoises as heavy as three people; crabs the size of cats . . . island giants are the fabric of legends—and nightmares. No one is sure why some island animals grow so big. It may be because there is less competition for food on an island or because there are fewer predators. In addition, larger species could be better equipped to survive the sea journey from the mainland.

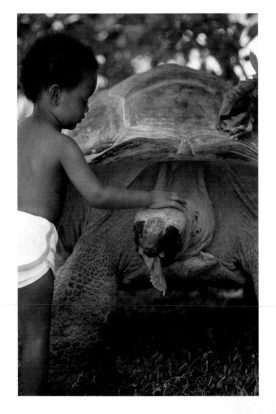

▲ As you can see, this giant tortoise from Fregate Island in the Seychelles is almost as tall as a small child. These tortoises were probably giants when they first reached the Seychelles, maybe by drifting on rafts of vegetation from the African island of Madagascar. Being large, with extra fat reserves, may help them survive the dry summer seasons, when there is often little food or water.

Long lives, large size

Certain reptiles, such as giant tortoises and the world's largest lizard, the Komodo dragon, never stop growing. On islands where there is a lot to eat and few predators reptiles can live for a long time, giving them years to grow to enormous sizes. The giant tortoises of the Galápagos Islands in the Pacific Ocean may live for more than 150 years, growing to more than 4 ft. (130cm) long.

My shell is my castle

Having the space to grow is important for the world's largest land crustacean—the coconut, or robber, crab. This giant is related to hermit crabs, which live inside empty shells to protect their soft abdomens (rear sections) but are then only able to grow as big as their home. Young coconut crabs also live inside empty shells for a few weeks, but the adults abandon these borrowed shelters, which means they can become much bigger. After they have left the shells they grow a hard case over their abdomens. When they outgrow this body casing, they molt and develop another, larger one.

Coconut trees grow well on islands, so the crabs have plenty of their favorite delicacy to eat, allowing them to reach 3 ft. (1m) from end to end.

Island feasts

Giant tortoises and coconut crabs are enormous, but they eat plants, not people. The Komodo dragon is not as harmless. Measuring up to 10 ft. (3m), it can kill large prey such as water buffalo and even the occasional unlucky human. There are no other big meat eaters on the islands where the dragon lives, probably because large mammals could not survive the long sea journey without food. This means that the dragon is the only big predator there and may have grown larger by eating the pygmy elephants that lived on the islands until recently.

▲ Standing so close to a Komodo dragon to get a good vacation photo is a high-risk activity. They are not fast animals and usually rely on surprise attacks to catch their prey. However, their sharp claws are lethal, and a mouth full of infectious bacteria means that even a small bite from a Komodo dragon can be fatal.

◄ Two coconut crabs tackle a coconut with their powerful claws. Coconuts are the favorite food of these huge crustaceans, and the crabs will go to great lengths to find one, even climbing trees to shake them to the ground. Coconut crabs get their alternative name of "robber" crabs because they steal anything they can lay their claws on.

Mighty serpents

Horrifying stories of giant man-eating snakes are common, but do such super-sized serpents really exist? The short answer is that there are very few records of snakes measuring much more than 29 ft. (9m), and even then researchers disagree about the exact lengths. Some sizable snakes, such as pythons and anacondas, are dangerous to people because of their enormity, but they do not usually attack humans. Really big snakes are not so common today because of habitat destruction and hunting.

The "big six"

The six biggest snakes are all boas and pythons. They are constricting snakes, which wrap their coils around their prey and kill them by suffocation. Two of these giants, the anaconda and the boa constrictor, come from South America. The Indian python and the reticulated python (or retic) come from Asia. The last two are the African rock python and the Amethystine, or scrub, python, which comes from Australia and New Guinea. Of the "big six," the longest is the retic, which can grow as long as a bus!

The heaviest snake is the anaconda, weighing up to 500 lbs. (227kg)—that is likely to be around five times heavier than a small human. Anacondas can grow to such massive sizes partly because they live in the rivers of the Amazon rain forest, where the water helps support their weight. They also keep growing (although at a slower rate) even when they are adults. This means that the real monsters are those that manage to escape from being killed, live for a long time, and grow to shocking sizes.

▶ The African rock python is the largest snake in Africa. This one is eating an antelope, which will provide the snake with enough energy to survive for several months. To help it swallow such a big meal, the snake unhinges its flexible jaws and allows its scaly body to stretch. Unlike humans, the python is able to breathe while swallowing because it pushes its windpipe to the front of its mouth.

▲ This enormous reticulated python needs five people to carry it. The retic is the longest snake in the world—it is widely accepted that it can reach a length of 29 ft. (9m), and many people claim to have seen larger sizes. The reticulated pattern of crisscross lines on the skin of the snake camouflages it well when it is hunting. Large retics may ambush animals as big as deer and pigs, and there are even occasional reports of humans on the menu . . .

Big appetites

It goes without saying that big snakes need to eat a lot. Finding food is not easy for an animal that has no legs and has to lie waiting for prey to come carelessly past. This is why large snakes live in places, such as rain forests, with plenty of food. There they can catch large prey, which sustains them for a long time. The anaconda, for example, can catch animals as big as caimans (see page 59), deer, and even jaguars in surprise attacks. Large snakes also live in places, such as swampy waterways, where they do not have to compete with big mammals for food.

Clever hunter

Pythons have an extra trick to help them find their prey. They have heat-sensitive pits, or holes, along their jaws, which allow them to sense the hot body of a nearby animal. This helps them find prey in the dark or among dense vegetation. Big pythons can catch prey as large as pigs, antelope, or even leopards. When any snake eats an enormous meal, its digestive system grows and becomes more efficient to help with the breakdown of food and to allow the snake to absorb as much of the goodness as possible.

Staying warm

A snake is cold-blooded. This means that its temperature varies with that of its surroundings, and it cannot keep its body warm all the time as humans do. A large snake takes longer to heat up than a small one, which is another reason why big snakes are found in tropical parts of the world. Their bodies need to be warm in order for them to stay active, and it would take them too long to heat up in a cold place. Spending time in water also helps some giant snakes maintain their body temperatures because the temperature of water is more constant than that of air.

Outsize insects

Insects are the most successful animals on Earth, yet most of them are less than one inch long. Their small size means they do not need much food and can live in tiny homes. Even the biggest insects are shorter than the width of this book when open.

▲ The prize for the longest beetle goes to *Titanus giganteus*, which grows up to 6 in. (16cm) long. It comes from the Amazon region of South America. Once the adult has emerged from its pupa, it lives for around three to four weeks but does not eat. The beetle defends itself with jaws that are strong enough to bite through a pencil. The male Hercules beetle is longer, measuring up to 7 in. (19cm), but half of its length is taken up by a long horn used for wrestling.

actual size

half actual size

◄ Shown here at around half its actual size, the African Goliath beetle is probably as big as your hand. It is thought to be the heaviest and bulkiest of all insects, but it is still a good flier. Males are usually heavier than females and weigh almost as much as an apple.

Take a big breath
One reason that insects do not grow to huge sizes is that their breathing systems would not work if their bodies were larger. Oxygen from the air enters an insect through holes along the sides of its body. The oxygen then passes through a system of branching tubes, called tracheae, and slowly seeps into the insect's body tissues. The bigger the insect, the farther the oxygen has to travel inside the body. So large insects usually have thin frames to make it easier for oxygen to reach all parts of the body. The more enormous insects are found in the tropics, where oxygen spreads into the body tissue more quickly. This is because higher temperatures allow oxygen to be absorbed easily.

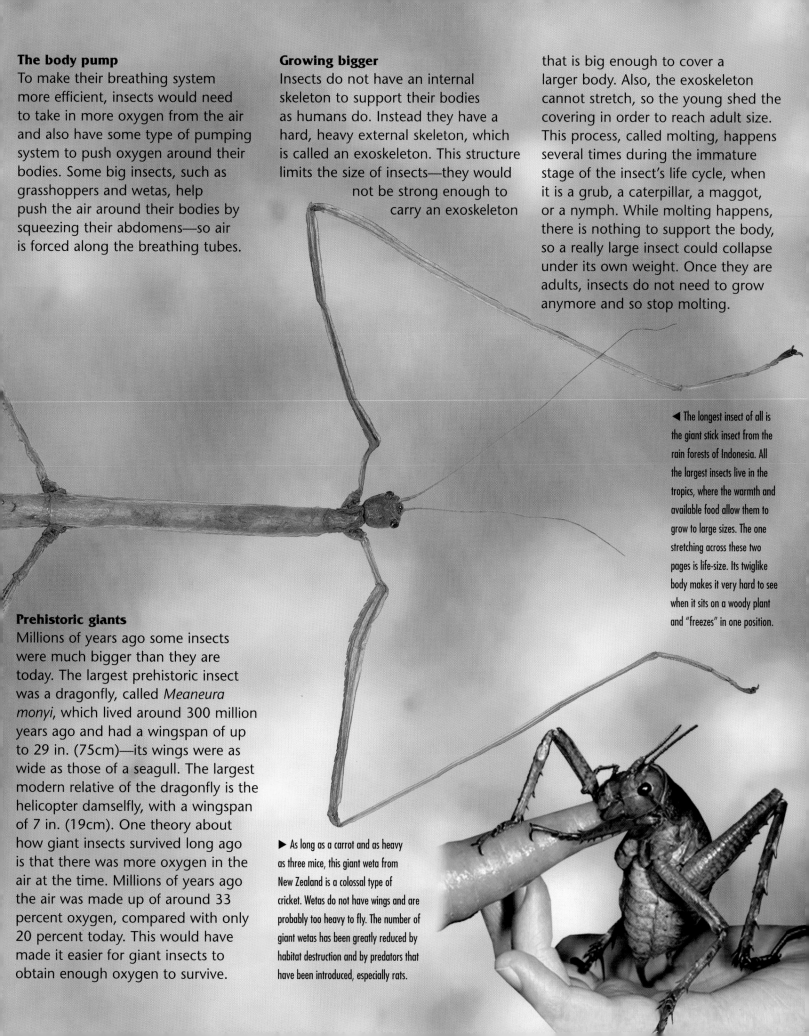

The body pump

To make their breathing system more efficient, insects would need to take in more oxygen from the air and also have some type of pumping system to push oxygen around their bodies. Some big insects, such as grasshoppers and wetas, help push the air around their bodies by squeezing their abdomens—so air is forced along the breathing tubes.

Growing bigger

Insects do not have an internal skeleton to support their bodies as humans do. Instead they have a hard, heavy external skeleton, which is called an exoskeleton. This structure limits the size of insects—they would not be strong enough to carry an exoskeleton that is big enough to cover a larger body. Also, the exoskeleton cannot stretch, so the young shed the covering in order to reach adult size. This process, called molting, happens several times during the immature stage of the insect's life cycle, when it is a grub, a caterpillar, a maggot, or a nymph. While molting happens, there is nothing to support the body, so a really large insect could collapse under its own weight. Once they are adults, insects do not need to grow anymore and so stop molting.

◄ The longest insect of all is the giant stick insect from the rain forests of Indonesia. All the largest insects live in the tropics, where the warmth and available food allow them to grow to large sizes. The one stretching across these two pages is life-size. Its twiglike body makes it very hard to see when it sits on a woody plant and "freezes" in one position.

Prehistoric giants

Millions of years ago some insects were much bigger than they are today. The largest prehistoric insect was a dragonfly, called *Meaneura monyi*, which lived around 300 million years ago and had a wingspan of up to 29 in. (75cm)—its wings were as wide as those of a seagull. The largest modern relative of the dragonfly is the helicopter damselfly, with a wingspan of 7 in. (19cm). One theory about how giant insects survived long ago is that there was more oxygen in the air at the time. Millions of years ago the air was made up of around 33 percent oxygen, compared with only 20 percent today. This would have made it easier for giant insects to obtain enough oxygen to survive.

► As long as a carrot and as heavy as three mice, this giant weta from New Zealand is a colossal type of cricket. Wetas do not have wings and are probably too heavy to fly. The number of giant wetas has been greatly reduced by habitat destruction and by predators that have been introduced, especially rats.

Colossal creepy crawlies

These giants look as though they could have come straight out of a scary movie—you definitely would not want to find one crawling on your bed! You might think of these mini giants as insects, but do not forget that there are plenty of creepy crawlies that are not insects. These range from giant centipedes and spiders to enormous worms and snails that are bigger than this page.

▲ Giant centipedes can give people a very painful bite because they inject a large amount of poisonous venom. However, their poison is not normally dangerous to healthy adult humans. Fortunately, giant centipedes, like this one, do not tend to bite people unless they are provoked. Because their bodies dry out easily, they usually come out at night, when the air is cool and damp.

Wingless wonders

Most insects have wings, and if their bodies were too big and heavy, they would not be able to fly. Creepy crawlies that are not insects, such as spiders, do not have to bother about being light enough to fly. They run, scurry, or slide along the ground or burrow beneath the soil, which means that some of them can grow to astounding sizes.

▶ Goliath tarantulas can grow as big as dinner plates, but their poison is not deadly to humans, and most are shy creatures. They can, however, flick their prickly hairs at an attacker. If these barbed hairs stick in the skin, they can cause exteme irritation.

Huge and venomous—a deadly combination

The largest creepy crawlies live in warm places where there is plenty to eat. Bigger creepy crawlies can naturally catch bigger prey, but they must also be efficient predators. Giant centipedes use their poisonous claws to paralyze prey as bulky as small birds. The biggest spider is the Goliath tarantula, also called the Goliath bird-eating spider. It has the strength to pounce on prey of its own size, injecting venom from hollow fangs. Its poison is not as strong as that from some smaller spiders, but its size and strength make it a force to be reckoned with.

Limits to growth

Like insects, the size of many creepy crawlies, such as centipedes and spiders, is limited by their breathing systems and by exoskeletons. They have to shed their exoskeleton in order to grow. Sometimes this only happens when the animal is young (as with most spiders), but molting and growth may also continue in adults as well. This allows some creepy crawlies, such as female tarantulas, to grow very big, especially if they live a long time. Female tarantulas may live for 20 years or more, molting occasionally to replace body parts (such as hairs) that have become damaged or worn out.

▲ The giant Gippsland earthworm from Australia is so big that it looks more like a snake than a worm. When stretched out, this giant can measure up to 13 ft. (4m)—that is probably three or four times as tall as you are! This earthworm is remarkable not just because it is a huge worm but also because it is a noisy worm. If you stomp on the ground above its burrow, it will become startled and slide rapidly through the tunnels of its earthy home, making a loud, distinct gurgling sound that you can hear more than 6 ft. (2m) above on the surface. The noise is caused by the worm sliding through a fluid that it produces to make the burrow walls slippery.

The biggest birds

The world's biggest birds are the ostrich of Africa, the emu and cassowary of Australasia, and the rhea of South America. These huge birds are all too heavy to fly, but they make up for it by being fantastic runners. The largest prehistoric birds were also flightless. They included the elephant bird of Madagascar—a slow-moving giant that weighed as much as a cow—and the giant moa of New Zealand, the tallest bird ever, which was as tall as two humans.

▲ The emu can grow to a height of more than 6 ft. (2m), making it Australia's tallest bird and the second-largest bird in the world after the ostrich. Emus spend most of the time feeding on fruits, grasses, flowers, seeds, and insects. In the fall the males eat as much as they can in order to build up fat reserves to last them through the breeding season. Male emus do not eat at this time because they sit permanently on their nests, incubating the eggs.

Raft birds

Ostriches, emus, rheas, cassowaries, and kiwis belong to a group of birds called the ratites. The name comes from the Latin word *ratis,* meaning "raft," and refers to the flat shape of their breastbones. Other features that ratites have in common include their small wings and fluffy feathers with no barbs, or hooks, which link the sides of each feather together and make them streamlined for flight.

What big eyes

The biggest bird alive today is the ostrich. This giant stands around 8 ft. (2.5m) tall—as high as a soccer goalpost—and has the biggest eyes (see page 7) of all land animals with backbones. An ostrich's sharp eyesight can spot predators and food up to 2 mi. (3.5km) away.

Long necks

Ostriches, emus, and rheas all have very long necks to help them see great distances over the grasslands where they live. The neck of the male ostrich can be as long as 5 ft. (1.5m)—it must be like having a built-in periscope. The flexible neck is also useful for reaching out for a wide range of food, such as leaves and seeds, on the ground and in bushes.

▲ The world's biggest birds also lay the most enormous eggs. The ostrich lays the largest eggs of any living bird. One egg is equal in volume to around 24 hens' eggs and can support the weight of a person. But flightless birds laid even bigger eggs in the past. The egg of the elephant bird (above, left) had a volume equivalent to 220 hens' eggs or nine ostrich eggs!

Speed and power

Except for the kiwi, ratites are all extremely big birds with large, muscular legs to run fast. The fastest sprinter of all, the ostrich, can run at speeds of up to 43 mph (70km/h)—faster than a horse. Most birds have three or four toes, but the ostrich has only two, reducing the amount of contact it has with the ground. This lessens the dragging effect of friction (a force that would slow the ostrich down), making it the fastest creature on two legs. High speed is useful for escaping predators since ratites cannot fly away. If a hungry carnivore does get close, the ostrich's powerful toes also make useful weapons. The kick of an ostrich can shatter a human skull, and people have been kicked to death by cassowaries protecting their young.

▲ The flightless giant moa from New Zealand could grow up to 12 ft. (3.7m) tall. It was also a ratite, like the elephant bird, emu, ostrich, rhea, cassowary, and kiwi. Moas were the only birds we know about that did not have any wings at all. Sadly, these extraordinary birds were much too easy for people to catch. The biggest moas were probably hunted to extinction by the end of the 1600s; however, some smaller species may have survived into the 1800s.

◄ Emus are champions of the marathon, covering great distances at a steady 4 mph (7km/h) in search of food and water. They can also sprint at speeds of up to 30 mph (48km/h).

giraffe

Predators and prey
It is useful for a predator to be big so that it can easily overpower its prey. On the other hand, prey animals, such as ostriches, are less likely to be killed if they are large. Being big has advantages for both predators and prey.

Eat and grow large
Large animals need a lot of food to keep their bodies working. Since warm, tropical places are home to the greatest variety of living things they have the most available food. This is why many enormous creatures, such as mega insects, live in tropical places. But any places with a good food supply may be home to animal giants. Kodiak bears, for example, live on a cold Alaskan island but still grow to big sizes on a diet of berries and salmon.

A long life
When an animal lives and grows for a long time, it can reach a remarkable size. Male elephants are usually larger than female elephants because they keep growing for longer than females. Reptiles keep growing all through their lives, and this has allowed some of them, such as the Komodo dragon and giant tortoises, to achieve huge proportions. Giant tortoises are one of the longest-living animals on Earth. Some may live up to 200 years.

Little and large
Insects and other creepy crawlies are unlikely to be the first animals that spring to mind when you think about giants. Even the most massive ones are still relatively small, probably because their external skeletons and breathing systems would not work in bigger bodies. However, a small size can be helpful. It means creepy crawlies can live in a range of places and eat all types of food, making them the most numerous and varied animals on Earth. There is not enough space and food on Earth for large numbers or a huge variety of giant animals to survive.

Go further . . .

For dinosaur information: www.dinodata.net

Find out about elephants: http://elephant.elehost.com

Watch slide shows and access all bear facts: www.bear.org

See some huge animals: www. extremescience.com/creatport.htm

African Animal Giants by Robert Cremins (National Geographic, 1997)

The Kingfisher Illustrated Dinosaur Encyclopedia by David Burnie (Kingfisher Publications, 2001)

Why Elephants Have Big Ears by Chris Lavers (St. Martin's Griffin, 2002)

Biologist
Studies living things. There are many branches of biology such as zoology (animals) and anatomy (structure).

Ecologist
Studies how living things are adapted to their environments and how they can be protected.

Paleontologist
Studies the fossilized remains of creatures that lived long ago.

Park ranger/zookeeper
Cares for animals in wildlife parks, nature reserves, or zoos.

Research scientist
Develops and tests theories.

Visit the dinosaurs and other giant animals at: American Museum of Natural History
Central Park West at 79th Street
New York, NY 10024-5192
Phone: (212) 769-5100
www.amnh.org

Observe animal giants at close range in a zoo or wildlife park such as:
San Diego Zoo
P. O. Box 120551
San Diego, CA 92112-0551
Phone: (619) 231-1515
www.sandiegozoo.org

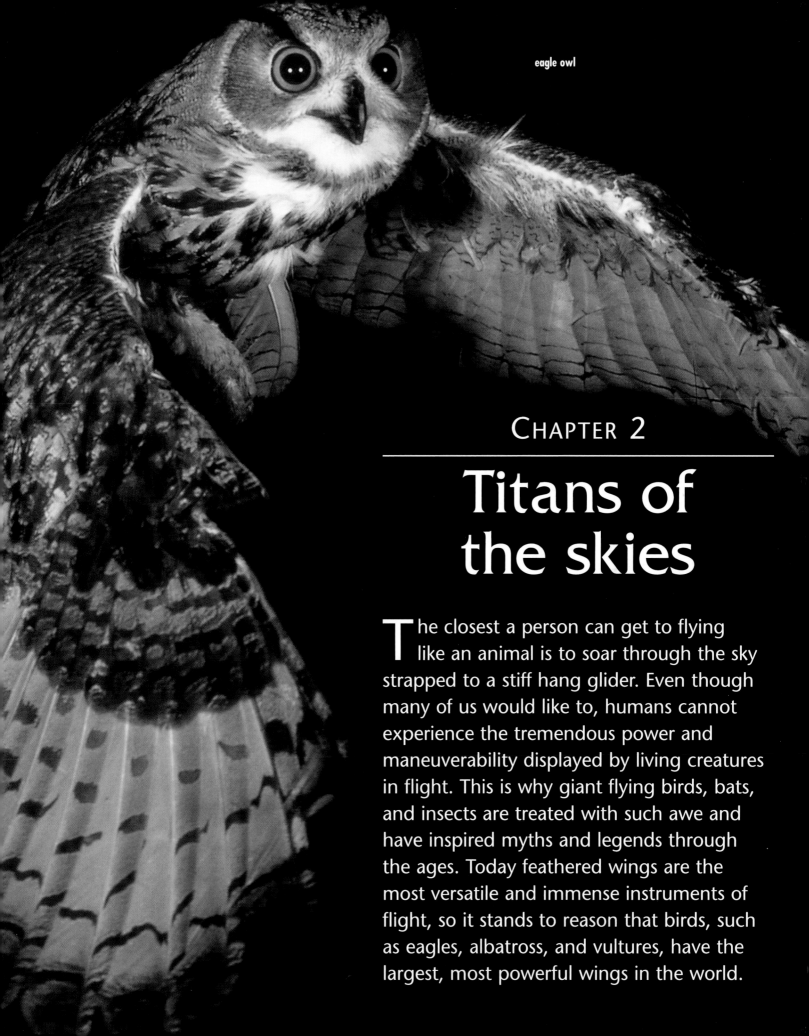

eagle owl

CHAPTER 2

Titans of the skies

The closest a person can get to flying like an animal is to soar through the sky strapped to a stiff hang glider. Even though many of us would like to, humans cannot experience the tremendous power and maneuverability displayed by living creatures in flight. This is why giant flying birds, bats, and insects are treated with such awe and have inspired myths and legends through the ages. Today feathered wings are the most versatile and immense instruments of flight, so it stands to reason that birds, such as eagles, albatross, and vultures, have the largest, most powerful wings in the world.

Giants of ancient skies

Dinosaurs were unable to fly, but pterosaurs, which were reptiles that may have been related to them, certainly could. In fact, they were the largest flying animals of all time. Pterosaurs lived alongside the dinosaurs for 165 million years and died out at the same time. The first pterosaurs were crow sized, with sharp, spiky teeth and long tails. Eventually these small pterosaurs became extinct, leaving pterodactyls, which were short-tailed pterosaurs, as the rulers of the skies. Some of the last pterodactyls became very large—one was the same size as a small airplane!

Lightweight giants

Pterosaurs had wings made of a double-sided sheet of skin supported by one extra-long finger and tough, flexible fibers, which helped stiffen the wings and maintain their shape. This structure is very similar to the wings of a bat, which are also made of skin but are more flexible and are supported by three or four fingers, not just one.

The skeleton of a pterosaur was lightweight, with thin-walled, hollow bones. This allowed faster, more efficient flight because the reptiles were not weighed down by heavy bodies. One of the largest pterosaurs, *Pteranodon*, had a 29 ft. (9m) wingspan and weighed around the same as a large swan or a pelican, the heaviest flying waterbirds alive today.

Gliders and flappers

The biggest pterosaurs had very long wings and were expert gliders, which saved energy. A number of them, including *Pteranodon*, may have lived like modern albatross, soaring over the sea in search of fish to eat. Smaller pterosaurs flew mainly by flapping their wings.

The wings were powered by large muscles and could swing backward and forward and rotate, as well as beating up and down. Pterosaurs could probably control their flight well, using their maneuverable wings, along with their fingers, skull crests, and the webs of skin between their feet, to help with steering and speed control. They probably flew fairly slowly, at similar speeds to today's birds and bats, which is no faster than 6–9 mph (10–15km/h), although some of the giant pterosaurs may have been able to fly as fast as 30 mph (50km/h). In all likelihood they were powerful fliers and may have migrated long distances in search of food or to avoid the seasonal changes in the weather.

▼ With a wingspan of up to 30 ft. (10m), *Quetzalcoatlus* was possibly the biggest of all the pterosaurs. Named after the winged serpent god of the Aztecs, it was almost twice the size of the largest-known modern flying bird. Unlike most pterosaurs, *Quetzalcoatlus* lived inland, not by the sea, and would have flown by soaring on rising currents of warm air, like today's vultures. It was probably a scavenger, feeding on the remains of dead dinosaurs with its toothless, daggerlike beak. Another idea is that it may have lived like a giant stork, wading through swamps to snap up frogs and other small animals.

Brains and hair

As well as having wings, pterosaurs had two other features that probably helped them become good fliers. One was their relatively large brains, which would have been needed in order to control the complex movements necessary for flight. The other was that they may have been warm-blooded, like bats and birds. A well-heated body would have kept their wing muscles warm enough to fly at all times. The remains of short, hairlike fibers have been found on the bodies of some pterosaur fossils. These provide evidence that pterosaurs were warm-blooded because the "hairs" would have helped them maintain a constant, warm body temperature.

The albatross

Soaring effortlessly over the windiest zones of the southern oceans, albatross are spectacular gliders. They can stay up in the air for hours without flapping their long, narrow wings. There are 14 species of albatross, but the three largest—the royal, wandering, and Amsterdam albatross—are called the great albatross and are the biggest seabirds of all. They have the greatest wingspans of any bird, measuring almost 10 ft. (3m) from one outstretched wing tip to the other.

Long-distance fliers

Albatross spend more than 90 percent of their lives gliding over the open oceans, sometimes covering several thousand miles in one day. In a lifetime they may fly almost 10 million mi. (16 million km). They come to land only to nest, usually on remote islands. For this reason they rely on the strength of their powerful wings to keep them in the air.

◄ Looking at British TV host Sir David Attenborough sitting beside a wandering albatross chick, you can see just how big it really is. Fluffy down feathers help keep the chick warm as it sits in the nest for almost ten months, often covered in snow from winter blizzards. A fully grown chick weighs around 27 lbs. (12kg), making it heavier than its parents and the largest chick of any seabird.

▶ Albatross have long inner wing bones with extra feathers attached. The wandering albatross has 88 flight feathers—more than any other bird. The long wings help it reach speeds of almost 55 mph (90km/h). In the breeding season wandering albatross parents may fly up to 93,000 mi. (150,000km) to find food for their chicks.

◀ In *The Rime of the Ancient Mariner* by the poet Samuel Taylor Coleridge a mariner (sailor) shoots and kills an albatross, bringing bad luck to his ship. The crew dies, but the mariner lives on, wearing the albatross around his neck as a reminder of his terrible deed. The albatross drops off only when the mariner learns to respect living things. Even then, he is condemned to wander forever, telling his story over and over again.

Champion gliders

The shape of an albatross's body is beautifully adapted for fast gliding. In addition to having extra-long wings, it has a streamlined body shaped like a torpedo and a short, square tail that acts like a rudder when changing direction. Its superb flying skills allow it to take advantage of rich areas of food that are far apart in the ocean. It can also turn some of the food it catches into a high-energy oil, which it stores in its stomach. It feeds this oil to its chicks, enabling the babies to survive for long periods of time without food. This gives the adults time to fly a long way to collect the next meal.

Sea fishers

Albatross feed mostly on squid, cuttlefish, small fish, and shrimplike animals, but they also eat the dead bodies of animals such as seals and penguins. Like their close relatives—the petrels, fulmars, and shearwaters—albatross have distinctive tube-shaped external nostrils, which they use partly to detect the smell of food. They often feed at night, when their prey comes to the water's surface. The birds usually dip their heads and powerful, hooked bills under the water to catch a meal, but some albatross, including the wandering and royal albatross, also dive below the surface in search of their prey.

Threats to survival

Many albatross and other seabirds are killed each year by a type of sea fishing called long-lining. Fishermen lay out lines that are up to 62 mi. (100km) long, dotted with thousands of baited hooks. The lines float on the surface, and the albatross swallow the hooks when they try to steal the bait. As the lines are pulled through the sea, the trapped birds are dragged underwater, and they drown. Several measures can be taken to save the albatross from this horrible death such as using bird-scaring devices and weighing down the lines so that the hooks sink quickly.

▼ To make the best use of the wind, albatross glide down to the surface of the sea and then turn into the wind, which blows them back up into the air again. By gliding up and down like this, they can keep flying for long periods of time without a single flap of their wings.

Wind

Sea level

Flight path

▶ The national bird of the U.S., the majestic bald eagle can measure up to 3 ft. (94cm) long. It has a varied diet of live prey such as fish, birds, and small mammals. A bald eagle can kill a large salmon that weighs as much as it does. Rough scales on its feet help it keep a firm hold of slippery fish, and its broad wings give it the power to lift up heavy prey. Bald eagles also scavenge for food and will even rob other birds, such as ospreys, of their catch whenever they can.

▼ The tallest bird of prey is the secretary bird. It stands up to 5 ft. (1.5m) tall, with a wingspan of more than 6 ft. (2m). Although this unusual-looking bird is a good flier, it spends most of the time on the ground. This is why its feet are adapted for walking instead of for grasping prey, and it has short, stubby toes instead of the long talons of other birds of prey. Secretary birds eat insects, small rodents, and snakes, killing the larger prey by stomping on it.

Birds of prey

The largest and most spectacular of the around 400 species of birds of prey are the enormous eagles and the vast vultures. The biggest of all is the Andean condor, a type of vulture that weighs around 33 lbs. (15kg) and has a wingspan of up to 10 ft. (3m). All vultures are scavengers, feeding on dead creatures instead of living prey. Their giant wings allow them to float high up in the sky without ever needing to flap them, covering huge distances as they search for their grisly supper. Eagles are more dignified hunters. The biggest eagles, such as the harpy eagle or the bald eagle, have wingspans of up to 6 ft. (2m) and are fierce and powerful, using their great size and strength to catch their prey.

Female heavyweights

Female birds of prey are often larger than males and are up to twice as heavy in some species. The greatest size difference is found in birds that both chase living prey and attack creatures that are very large in relation to their own size. No one is sure why the female is bigger than the male, but it could be in order to give her more energy to lay her eggs and to protect her young.

◀ The legendary roc, or rukh, was supposed to be strong enough to carry off elephants to feed to its young. The roc may have been based on either a large Madagascan eagle or the elephant bird, which lived on the island of Madagascar, off the coast of southern Africa (see pages 24–25). Both of these giant birds are now extinct.

Cleanup crew

The huge, broad wings of a vulture allow it to glide up into the sky and drift on rising currents of hot air or strong winds. With their sharp eyesight, vultures can spot prey from several miles away, but most find food by watching other vultures. If one bird notices a carcass, it begins to circle lower and lower. This is the signal for nearby vultures to join in the feast. Some vultures eat so much at one time that they are too heavy to fly for a while afterward.

Terrible talons

Eagles work harder than vultures to get their meals. They, too, have sharp eyesight, but their prey is alive, and they need powerful wings to pursue, catch, and carry it. They kill with their strong feet, driving huge, razor-sharp talons, like a ring of spears, into their victims. They then carry away the prey in these claws and eat it in peace.

At 10 lbs. (4.5kg), the female harpy eagle is the strongest, heaviest eagle in the world today. She can kill prey that weighs as much as she does.

Extinct giant

The largest eagle ever was the Haast's eagle, which lived in New Zealand until around 500 years ago. Females weighed up to 29 lbs. (13kg) and had talons as big as a tiger's claws. These giants ate moas (see page 25), which were often 20 times heavier than the eagles were. Today most eagles attack prey that is light enough to carry since they have to take it to a safe place to eat. There were no other large predators in New Zealand, so the Haast's eagle could attack, kill, and eat on the spot.

Creatures of the night sky

While we are asleep in our beds at night, a whole army of owls, bats, and insects is swooping through the darkness, intent on finding a meal or a mate. The giants of this nocturnal world include owls as big as a small child and fruit bats with wingspans as wide as your outstretched arms. Large, powerful wings enable these two types of night fliers to find plenty of food, and this, in turn, allows them to grow to giant sizes.

Super owls

The biggest owls are the northern eagle owl, the great gray owl, and the snowy owl. These magnificent creatures have a body size of 23–27 in. (60–70cm) and wingspans of more than 5 ft. (1.5m). Female owls are often up to 25 percent larger than males, probably so that they are better equipped to lay eggs and protect their young.

All of these owls live in the extensive northern forests of North America and Asia and in the cold, bare tundra lands, where their large size may help them stay warm. In the forests and on the tundra there are plenty of mammals and birds to eat. Despite their great size, the super owls eat many small mammals such as voles and lemmings. As the populations of these mammals go up and down, so do the numbers of the owls that eat them.

Night owls

To help them hunt in the dark, owls have exceptional hearing and eyesight. Their large eyes may account for up to five percent of their overall body weight. The largest owls have eyes that are around the same size as those of a person, but they can see in the dark two to three times better than a human. Their eyes are not ball shaped, like human eyes, but are huge tubes that go straight back into the head and are held in place by bony structures. This means owls cannot move their eyes. To compensate for this, they have long, flexible necks, which allow them to turn their heads almost completely around in a full circle to look to the sides and behind their bodies.

▲ Owls, such as this great horned owl, have large eyes and huge pupils to let in as much light as possible. An owl's eyes gather possibly 100 times more light than a pigeon's eyes, which means the owl can see over greater distances and much more clearly, especially in the dark. An owl also has extra eyelids, which clean and protect the surface of the eyes.

▼ Northern eagle owls are very powerful predators, able to kill mammals as big as young deer. Like all owls, they have fluffy fringes on their flight feathers, which muffle the sound of their wings. Their silent flight allows them to hear their prey and then to sneak up for an attack without being heard. To grasp and kill prey they have immensely strong legs and feet armed with needle-sharp talons. They carry small prey in their beaks, but larger prey has to be carried in the talons.

Mega bats and micro bats

Did you know that around one fourth of all mammals are bats? There are two main groups of bats: the 700 or so species of small, insect-eating micro bats and the roughly 170 species of much larger and slower mega bats. The micro bats' short wings, which they flap 11–18 times per second, make them terrific fliers, twisting and turning through the air as they scoop up night-flying insects. Larger wings would slow them down and make it difficult for them to catch their prey.

The mega bats do not need to chase their food because they feed on fruit. To find trees with enough food growing on them, they have to fly long distances through tropical forests, so they tend to have much larger wings. Their giant wings make them slow but powerful fliers and can carry them up to 9 mi. (15km) in one night in their search for a fruity dinner.

▲ The giant Indian fruit bat is the biggest bat in the world, with a wingspan of around 5 ft. (1.5m) and a body weight of up to 3 lbs. (1.3kg). This mega bat is also called the Indian flying fox because its furry face resembles a fox's face. During the day the giant fruit bat roosts in trees in a huge colony, which can number up to several thousand bats. At night it flies great distances on the hunt for fruit such as mangoes, bananas, papayas, and figs.

giant Indian fruit bat   eagle owl/ great horned owl

Butterflies and moths

Is it a bird? Is it a plane? No—it's supermoth! The Hercules moth (center) is as big as the one on this page in real life. The biggest butterfly in the world is just as large. It is called the Queen Alexandra's birdwing butterfly because its wings are as wide as those of a bird. Despite their huge size, these giant butterflies and moths are lightweight creatures, so they are not too heavy to fly.

Large ladies

The biggest moths and butterflies in the world are all females. This might be so that they have more energy to develop and lay their eggs. Bigger moths and butterflies are easier for predators to see; this could be why the females are not very colorful. Their camouflage makes them much less visible than males and gives them a better chance of laying their eggs in safety. The brown wings of the female Queen Alexandra's birdwing contrast sharply with the shiny blue-and-green wings of the male (see page 60). The males' colors may warn predators to leave them alone because they are poisonous or might help make them more attractive to females. The huge size and beautiful wings of the Queen Alexandra's birdwing butterflies certainly made them very attractive to butterfly collectors in the past. In fact, so many of the butterflies were collected from the wild that these stunning giants are now very rare.

Little and large

Butterflies and moths come in a huge range of sizes. The female Queen Alexandra's birdwing is around 25 times the size of the world's smallest butterfly, the dwarf blue butterfly of South Africa. This tiny cousin has a wingspan of less than one inch, compared to the 11 in. (28cm) wingspan of the female Queen Alexandra's birdwing butterfly. The smallest moth, *Stigmella ridiculosa*, has a wingspan of only 0.08 in. (2mm). It looks like a dot next to the moth with the largest wingspan, the giant Agrippa moth, which measures 12 in. (30cm) from one wing tip to the other.

▼ This female Hercules moth has a wingspan of more than 10 in. (27cm) and is one of the largest moths in the world. Only the female Atlas moth, which looks very similar, is slightly bigger in overall size. All giant moths and butterflies have fairly small bodies—the impression of size comes from their tremendous wingspan. The big species all live in tropical habitats, such as rain forests, where there is enough sunshine to warm up their flight muscles so that they can flap their gigantic wings. Female Hercules moths live for only a few days, relying on the energy from fat stored by the caterpillar to keep them moving.

▼ Looking at this *Milionia doheityi* moth next to the Hercules moth really brings home the enormity of the giant. Both species live in the same habitat—the tropical rain forests of Papua New Guinea, a group of islands in the Pacific Ocean.

actual size

Living in harmony

One reason for this great variation in size is that big species live in different places than small species, which means that they can share the resources available in any habitat. The giant birdwing butterflies flap lazily around at the tops of rain-forest trees using their powerful wings, while the caterpillars of some of the tiniest moths live inside leaves, flowers, seeds, and fruits.

Big caterpillars

Adult butterflies and moths never grow, and the female Hercules moth does not even eat. They grow only at the caterpillar stage, which means that a large adult must develop from a huge caterpillar. The young crawler spends its life eating, but its skin does not grow as fast as its body. This means that every so often the caterpillar develops a new, bigger skin and sheds, or molts, the old one. As the old skin splits, the caterpillar wiggles out, swallowing air to expand and stretch its body. When a caterpillar is fully grown, it changes into a pupa. Inside this protective case the parts of the caterpillar's body are broken down and rebuilt into the adult butterfly or moth. The adult's wings are folded up inside the pupa. They do not expand until the adult emerges into the world and pumps blood into its wing veins in order to stiffen and flatten the wings. It may take more than two hours for a big butterfly to expand its wings.

▲ The warm temperatures and good food supplies in the rain-forest home of the caterpillar of the Hercules moth help it grow up to an enormous 6.6 in. (17cm) long. Its large, fat body would make a tasty meal for any predator, but luckily it is protected by rows of sharp, yellow spikes along its back.

Indian giant fruit bat

Lightweight fliers

The bodies of flying animals cannot be too heavy, or they would never get off the ground, even with very powerful wings. If you have ever had a giant butterfly or moth land on your hand, you will have felt how light they are, despite their size.

Even the largest birds, such as giant owls, are not very heavy because of their thin-walled, hollow bones, some of which have air sacs inside to make them lighter.

Saving energy

Flying is tiring and uses up a lot of energy. But long or wide wings, such as those of albatross, vultures, or giant fruit bats, allow effortless gliding. This makes it easier to fly long distances to find food or to avoid bad weather.

Warm wings

Wing muscles need to be warm in order for an animal to fly. Birds and bats are warm-blooded, so they have warm bodies all the time. This means they can fly whenever they need to. Pterosaurs may also have had warm bodies, which would probably have helped them develop their flying skills. On the other hand, insects like butterflies and moths have bodies that warm up and cool down with their surroundings—they are cold-blooded. They can only fly when their wing muscles are warm enough—and the muscles needed for big wings need a lot of warming up. This is one reason why large flying insects live in warm tropical places such as rain forests.

Massive moms

Female fliers are often even more gigantic than their male partners. The largest butterfly in the world is a female, and some female birds of prey are up to twice as heavy as their mates. No one is sure why this is, but it may help the females lay their eggs and to defend and feed their young.

Go further . . .

All about owls: www.owlpages.com

Find out about albatross: www.birdlife.net/action/campaigns

For answers to pterosaur questions: www.bbc.co.uk/dinosaurs/ dig_deeper/faq_pterosaur.shtml

Facts about bats: www.batcm.org

Monsters: The World's Most Incredible Animals by Beatrice Fontanel (Peter Bedrick Books, 2000)

Raptor! A Kid's Guide to Birds of Prey by Christina Laubach (Storey Books, 2003)

Entomologist
Specializes in the study of insects.

Falconer
Keeps and trains birds of prey, especially hawks, and may fly them in displays for the public.

Museum worker
Classifies species (taxonomist), organizes museum collections, and prepares exhibitions (curator).

Ornithologist
Studies the biology of birds.

Wildlife photographer
Photographs wildlife for books, magazines, museums, television, videos, or web sites.

Learn about eagles, hawks, falcons, and other birds of prey at: The Raptor Center of the University of Minnesota 1620 Fitch Avenue St. Paul, MN 55108 Phone: (612) 624-4745 www.raptor.cvm.umn.edu

Meet some tropical butterflies at: Butterfly World Tradewinds Park 3600 W. Sample Road Coconut Creek, FL 33073 Phone: (954) 977-4400 www.butterflyworld.com

CHAPTER 3

Giants of the water

Giant animals that swim through the waters of oceans, rivers, and lakes have a huge advantage over animals that fly through the air or walk across land. The water pushes up their bodies, helping support their huge weights. Today high levels of oxygen in deep freshwater lakes and cold oceans allow animals to release more energy from their food and may enable them to grow bigger. Water is also home to a large variety of living things, providing plenty of food for animals to grow to mammoth measurements. The biggest animal the world has ever known—the blue whale—lives in the oceans, along with other goliaths of the sea such as monstrous squid, jumbo jellyfish, and stupendous sharks. It is possible that even more giants lurk in the darkness of the deep oceans. Would you like to be the one to discover them?

whale shark

Giants of ancient waters

A whole host of giant predatory reptiles swam through ancient seas and oceans. The earliest of these were large ichthyosaurs such as *Temnodontosaurus*; then followed enormous pliosaurs such as *Liopleurodon* and *Kronosaurus*; and finally massive mosasaurs such as *Mosasaurus* and *Tylosaurus*. Some of these marine giants measured more than 33 ft. (10m) in length, and a few may have been as long as 65 ft. (20m)—as big as a sperm whale. The bodies of these enormous creatures were buoyed up by the water, and there was plenty of food in the sea to enable them to grow to outsize proportions.

Predators of a different class

Ancient marine reptiles were much more dangerous than most of today's aquatic giants. The pliosaurs were colossal, and the biggest among them would have been powerful enough to bite a medium-sized modern car in half! They had huge heads, possibly measuring up to 13 ft. (4m) long, lined with rows of sharp teeth at least as big as bananas. Large, powerful muscles drove these biting teeth into the prey.

Around 70 million years ago mosasaurs took over from the pliosaurs as the top predators and became the most dangerous creatures in the oceans. Mosasaurs were probably distant relatives of today's monster monitor lizards, such as the Komodo dragon (see page 17), and maybe even snakes as well. Several mosasaurs reached lengths of almost 50 ft. (15m), while one giant, *Hainosaurus bernardi*, was 56 ft. (17m) long. Their unusual jaws could bend sideways to surround and crush their prey, which they then swallowed whole, eating in the same way as a modern snake.

▼ *Elasmosaurus* had the longest neck in proportion to its body of any known animal, beating even the giraffe. With at least 71 bones for support, its neck could grow up to 20 ft. (6m) long. This allowed *Elasmosaurus* to launch a surprise attack without even moving its body by suddenly reaching into a school of fish from several feet away.

Seeing in the dark

Ichthyosaurs (meaning "fish lizards") were reptiles that looked like modern dolphins and followed a similar fish-eating lifestyle. Unlike dolphins, which are mammals, ichthyosaurs had back flippers as well as front ones, and their tails were vertical instead of horizontal. Ancient ichthyosaurs could have had eyeballs that measured around 1 ft. (30cm) across—as wide as bowling balls. This is even bigger than the eyes of today's giant squid, which are the largest of any living creature. Big eyes can let in and detect more light, so they would have helped ancient ichthyosaurs hunt hundreds of feet below the surface of the ocean, where it is extremely dark.

Water babies

The biggest marine reptiles could not come onto land to lay eggs. They would have suffered like beached whales, unable to move and condemned to die by overheating or from suffocation caused by the collapse of their lungs. There is fossil evidence of mosasaurs and ichthyosaurs giving birth to live young in the water, and it is likely that other large marine reptiles reproduced in the same way.

The blue whale

Gliding through the world's oceans is the most famous giant of all—the blue whale. Reaching lengths of more than 98 ft. (30m) and weights of 150 tons or more, this monumental giant is the largest animal in the world—the longest one on record measured a staggering 110 ft. (33.58m). Blue whales today are not as large as they were in the past because the biggest ones have been killed for their meat and blubber. Despite being a protected species, they are still endangered by pollution, hunting, and being trapped in fishnets. The sad consequence of this is that there are now probably fewer than 8,000 blue whales left.

Speedy swimmer

The combination of a smooth body, a slim, streamlined shape, and 18-ft. (5.5-m)-wide tail flukes (fins) makes a blue whale a powerful swimmer. It can reach speeds of up to 31 mph (50km/h), although it usually cruises at 3–12 mph (5–20km/h) without using too much energy. Blue whales are too fast and too big to be caught by most ocean predators, with the exception of packs of killer whales and humans.

Giant gulper

The blue whale feeds mostly on tiny, shrimplike animals called krill (a type of plankton), which are less than 2 in. (5cm) long and drift in huge bunches close to the surface of the oceans. A blue whale plunges into a mass of krill with its mouth wide open, speedily gulping a mouthful of food and water. Inside its cavernous mouth hundreds of stiff strips of baleen hang down from the top jaw. Baleen is made from the same material as human fingernails and has fringes of hair along the edges. As the whale uses its throat muscles and tongue to force water out of its mouth, the baleen plates act as sieves, trapping huge amounts of krill on the hairy fringes. The krill is then swallowed down the whale's throat, which is unexpectedly tiny.

▼ One of the main reasons the blue whale has been able to reach such gigantic proportions is that seawater helps support its body. If it were stranded on land, a blue whale would die—at around 22 tons, the bones of its skeleton cannot support the weight of its body in the air, so the whole thing would collapse, crushing its soft internal organs. Its jaws are up to 24 ft. (7.3m) long—the largest in the animal kingdom.

◄ A blue whale's mouth expands when it feeds because it has loose folds of skin, which look like pleats, running down from its chin almost to its belly button. As these pleats open up, they increase the mouth size, a lot like a musician opening an accordion.

▲ We know very little about the social life of blue whales, but they are usually seen alone or in small groups of two to four individuals. This might be because they need large feeding areas all to themselves. Blue whales make very loud sounds (as the loudest animals on Earth, the whistles made by these creatures are louder than a jet engine), which may help whales that are far apart stay in touch. The echoes of these loud sounds may also help blue whales find food and navigate their way through the oceans.

World's biggest babies

At birth, baby blue whales weigh at least 2.5 tons—700 times the weight of a human baby. They grow quickly because their mothers feed them up to 78 gal. (300L) of fatty milk every day. A mother blue whale loses around one third of her body weight over the eight months that she feeds her calf. This may be one reason why females are bigger than males—this gives them enough fat reserves to survive feeding their babies. Even though baby blue whales stop drinking their mother's milk when they are eight months old, they do not mature into adults and become able to reproduce for at least ten years. No one knows how long they live, but scientists think they could reach 60 to 70 years old. This is just one of the many details left to be discovered about these beautiful and gentle creatures.

Mammoth sea mammals

The blue whale might be of unrivaled size, but it is by no means the only giant of its class. In a competition for most mammoth marine mammal there would also be a few other contenders for the top places. First behind the blue whale would be the other whales such as humpback and sperm whales. Second would be the elephant seal and the walrus (see page 61), the largest pinnipeds. In third place would be the West Indian manatee and the dugong, or sea cow, which are the largest sirenians.

▲ The largest recorded West Indian manatee was a female that reached a length of 13 ft. (4.1m). Manatees do not have true blubber, just a thick skin and a fat layer that provides poor insulation against the cold. They live mainly in the warm tropical coastal and inland waters of the world. Manatees are very efficient herbivores, which helps them grow to big sizes. Their huge mouths are good at grasping and uprooting water plants. They also extract as much energy as they can from their food before it passes out of their bodies.

Fatty food

One reason that the biggest whales and seals are so large is that their bodies are surrounded by thick layers of fatty blubber, which may be more than 9 in. (25cm) thick. The blubber makes their bodies streamlined, stops body heat from escaping when they swim in very cold polar oceans, and also acts as a food supply during the breeding season, when they may not be able to feed. For around one month, while they are feeding their pups on rich milk, female elephant seals do not eat. Male elephant seals do not eat in the breeding season either, since they are constantly defending their harem of females against rival males. They may lose up to half of their body weight in a three-month season. Migrant whales, such as gray, blue, and humpback whales, also don't eat much during the winter breeding season, which they spend in warmer tropical waters. They use the energy they stored as body fat in the summer when they were feeding in cold polar waters.

Cruisers and chasers

Toothed whales, such as sperm whales, are usually much smaller than baleen whales, such as humpback whales, which filter tiny drifting plankton out of the water with fringed plates called baleen. Baleen whales do not have to do much active swimming in order to feed themselves. They just cruise along scooping up plankton, swallowing millions of the small animals during one meal. Toothed whales, on the other hand, must chase their prey, and larger sizes could really slow them down. They catch and swallow bigger animals, such as fish, one at a time. Most toothed whales, including dolphins and white, or beluga, whales, are 10–20 ft. (3–6m) long. But the largest toothed whale, the sperm whale, may reach a length of almost 70 ft. (20m).

◄ Male elephant seals are at least three times heavier than females. When threatened by male rivals or, as seen in this picture, a scientist recording a roar, a male will lift up the front half of its body and bellow loudly, inflating its nose and using it like a loudspeaker to make more noise.

◄ A fearless tussock, around as long as a person's hand, pecks for food scraps right on the nose of a female elephant seal. The females have much smaller noses than male elephant seals and lead much quieter lives.

Lurking crocodiles

Survivors from the age of the dinosaurs, crocodiles are superbly adapted to their environment. They lurk lazily in the water, waiting to snap up prey in their huge jaws. The biggest jaws of all belong to the largest reptile in the world—the saltwater crocodile. It weighs as much as three cars and grows over three times longer than a bed! Almost as immense—and just as threatening— is the largest freshwater predator in Africa—the Nile crocodile.

Little babies, awesome adults

When a baby crocodile hatches from its egg, it is so small that you could easily hold one in your hand. A mother crocodile holds her young in her mouth to keep them safe and to carry them from their nest to the water. She can carry up to 20 young at a time like this. The babies grow very quickly. If they have enough to eat, they can grow almost 1 ft. (30cm) per year until they are around 15 years old. Then they keep growing at a much slower rate for the rest of their lives. In captivity crocodiles grow faster than they do in the wild because they are kept in warm water and have plenty to eat.

Lazy eaters

Saltwater and Nile crocodiles are so big that they can catch large animals, such as zebras, cows, buffalo, and horses, but they mostly eat a lot of fish. They sometimes attack humans, although this usually happens only when people disturb them, especially during the mating and nesting seasons. Most crocodiles are timid and avoid people whenever possible. Normally crocodiles sit and wait for their food to come to them because this saves energy. This sort of lazy lifestyle, along with the fact that they can store energy from their food in their tails and other parts of the body, allows a big crocodile to survive for up to two years between meals. Since they warm up and cool down with their surroundings they do not need to use energy to stay warm, as mammals and birds do.

Survival

Almost 200 million years ago crocodiles looked very similar to today's species. Apart from birds, they are the closest living relatives of dinosaurs. Crocodiles have survived for so long and have grown to such large sizes because they are very well suited to their lifestyles. They also seem to be good at fighting diseases and rarely develop cancers. Sadly, almost half of all crocodile species are endangered by loss of habitat, illegal hunting, and trapping. Very large crocodiles are now rare because they are killed before they grow to their maximum size.

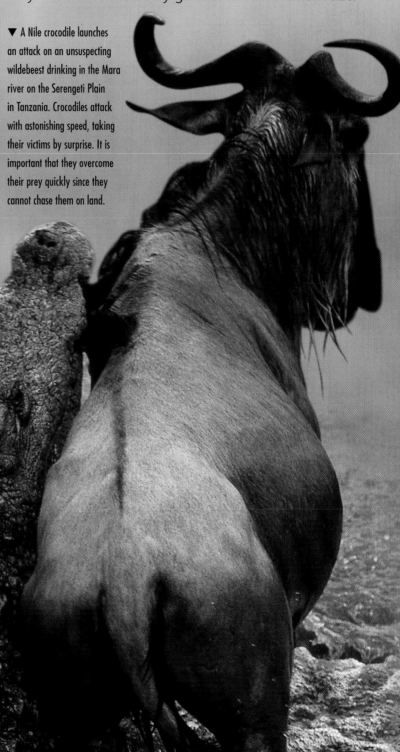

▼ A Nile crocodile launches an attack on an unsuspecting wildebeest drinking in the Mara river on the Serengeti Plain in Tanzania. Crocodiles attack with astonishing speed, taking their victims by surprise. It is important that they overcome their prey quickly since they cannot chase them on land.

◄ This saltwater, or estuarine, crocodile is basking in shallow water, allowing a good view inside its gaping jaws. Crocodiles have two to three times as many teeth as a person, but these cannot be used to chew food, so they swallow it whole or tear it into chunks.

Amazing amphibians

Frogs, toads, newts, and salamanders are all amphibians, which means "a being with a double life." Most of them live part of their lives in the water, usually when young, and the rest on land when they grow up. They can breathe through their skin as well as, or instead of, using their lungs. Some, usually the young, have gills for breathing underwater. Amphibians tend to be small, secretive animals, but there are a few giants that break all the records!

▲ The chunky African bullfrog grows to a length of around 8 in. (20cm) from its snout to the end of its body. It has a very wide, gaping mouth, which allows it to catch large prey, especially other frogs.

▼ The Chinese giant salamander looks like a monster from a science-fiction movie. It has a broad, flat head with no eyelids. The ridge of wrinkled skin increases the surface area for absorbing oxygen from the water of its mountain-stream habitat.

Giant salamanders
The biggest amphibians of all are two species of giant salamanders, the Chinese and the Japanese giant salamanders. The Chinese giant salamander is the bigger of the two. One outstanding individual was the size of a small crocodile! Average adults measure 3.7 ft. (1.14m) in length and weigh around 55–66 lbs. (25–30kg)—that is as much as a child. One reason the salamanders grow so big might be because their body processes work very slowly, saving energy and allowing them to grow larger over time. Another reason for their size is that they live a long time—one Japanese giant survived for 55 years in captivity. Unfortunately, the salamanders are hunted for food and for use in traditional medicines, so they are now rare.

▶ The body of the giant cane toad measures up to 12 in. (30cm) — this is around ten times bigger than the smallest toad, the oak toad. Adults have large poison glands on their shoulders and smaller ones all over the body. Their poison can kill mammals, such as dogs, and is harmful to humans, especially small children.

◀ The Goliath frog is the world's largest frog. It was once common in the rivers of tropical western Africa. Today these amphibians are threatened by extinction as a result of habitat destruction and excessive hunting.

Monster frog

Around 90 percent of the world's amphibians are frogs and toads. In contrast to salamanders, which have long tails, frogs and toads have no tails at all. The difference between frogs and toads is not distinct. Frogs usually have smooth skin, long back legs, webbed feet, and live by water. They move by hopping, although some can climb trees. Toads have a more warty skin than frogs and prefer to live on the ground, moving by crawling.

Most frogs would fit into the palm of your hand, but there is a real giant with a body longer than this page. Called the Goliath frog, the largest one ever recorded measured 2.85 ft. (87.63cm), including its very long legs. It weighed as much as a large pet cat! The Goliath frog comes from warm places in western Africa, where there is plenty of food to enable it to grow to huge proportions.

The toads' new abode

The biggest toad in the world is the cane, or marine, toad. Females often weigh more than a bag of sugar and, in captivity, may reach a length of 9 in. (24cm) and a weight of 5.5 lbs. (2.5kg). These huge toads originally came from tropical South America but were introduced into Australia to eat pests that were destroying the sugar-cane crops. Unfortunately, there were few predators in Australia to eat the toads, so their numbers grew fast. In some areas they have reached plague proportions, carpeting roads in the thousands. As well as eating the insect pests, the cane toads eat a lot of the native wildlife. Introducing animals from one country to another can have terrible consequences, especially when they are giants with huge appetites.

Mega sharks

If you thought that the biggest sharks are also the most dangerous hunters, you would be wrong. The great white shark, a truly dangerous creature, is one third of the size of the most immense shark in the world, the whale shark. Equal in mass to two buses, this fish is a genuine giant.

Gentle giants

The whale shark is not only the most gargantuan of all sharks, it is the biggest fish, too. The most enormous one ever recorded was 44 ft. (13.5m). The second-largest fish is also a shark, the basking shark, which grows up to 40 ft. (12m) long. Even though they are big enough to swallow humans whole, these gentle giants are harmless.

A matter of size

Strangely, the most gigantic fish eat the tiniest creatures in the sea! Both the whale shark and the basking shark feed mostly on plankton (tiny plants and animals that drift close to the water's surface). Plankton is rich in energy because it is at the beginning of the food chain, much like grass is on land.

The great white shark feeds on fish and seals, which are farther up the food chain. Energy is lost at each link in the chain as it is used to fuel the life processes of the animal doing the eating. This means that there is less energy left for the great white shark, so it cannot grow as large as a basking or whale shark.

Feeding habits

The plankton eaters use very little energy to catch their food, which is another reason why they can reach such big sizes. They open their large mouths to let in water and then sieve food from the water as it flows back out over their gills. The food is trapped on a fine net of filters, a little like combs, that are attached to the gills. Almost nothing but water gets through these filters. The basking shark filters more than 375,000 gal. (1.5 million L) of water in one hour. That is as much water as there is in an Olympic-size swimming pool!

◄ Great white sharks attack using a high-speed dash and are powerful enough to eat a whole seal in one bite. Attacks on people may happen because the shark mistakes them for seals.

◀ This snorkeler must have had a shock when he looked below the surface! Whale sharks are harmless to people. The only danger is being scraped by their rough skin, which is like sandpaper, or being knocked by a sideways sweep of their huge tails.

▶ This plankton is the type of food that the larger sharks eat. It is made up of microscopic plants along with minuscule, shrimplike animals, tiny worms, fish eggs, and the young of crabs and barnacles.

Phenomenal fish

Except for sharks, the biggest fish range from the weighty ocean sunfish, which can top two tons, to the oarfish, which is able to grow as long as four cars. There is plenty of food in their aquatic environment to sustain these giants, and the water supports their immense bodies. These factors, along with their fast growth and long life spans, mean that super sizes are easily achievable for water dwellers. Unfortunately, their size also makes them attractive to human predators, so numbers of big fish, such as tuna, have declined dramatically in recent years.

▲ The largest ray, the manta ray, usually has a wingspan of up to 23 ft. (7m), but the largest recorded width is around 30 ft. (9m). Its nickname is "devil ray" because of the hornlike fins on its head. Like the whale shark and blue whale, mantas are gentle, plankton-eating giants.

Plankton harvest

Many giant ocean fish, including the manta ray, feed on tiny plants and animals called plankton, which drift in abundance close to the sea's surface. Plankton is full of energy and is easy to catch, which makes it possible for large fish that eat it to develop and grow. *Leedsichthys*, the largest fish ever to have swum in the oceans, was a plankton feeder. It lived during the time of the giant dinosaurs, around 155 million years ago, and could have reached a length of 49–98 ft. (15–30m). No one has yet discovered a complete skeleton of this monster fish, so it is difficult to be sure about its actual size.

Ever smaller

Beluga sturgeons of the Caspian Sea are on the verge of extinction owing to pollution of their water habitat and overfishing for their valuable eggs, which are called caviar when preserved in salt. In the past beluga sturgeon weighing more than 2,200 lbs. (1,000kg) were recorded, but average weights today are as low as 44 lbs. (20kg).

Disappearing sea giants

In the last 50 years so many fish have been caught that 50–90 percent of some large species have disappeared completely. The problem is that many fish are killed when they are young, before they are able to reproduce and build up the next generation. In addition, modern fishing methods are so efficient that nets and lines used to catch one type of fish trap and kill many other, unwanted sea creatures.

◄ This woman might make it look easy to carry a tuna, but do not be fooled! An average weight for a tuna is up to 100 lbs. (45kg), and some giant tuna can weigh more than 397 lbs. (180kg), with a maximum weight of around 1,300 lbs. (600kg)—around 15 times your weight. These remarkable fish grow rapidly and live as long as 30 years, which enables them to reach gigantic proportions. The only predators that dare to attack these tremendous tuna are some sharks, whales, and people.

▼ The ocean sunfish is the world's heaviest and broadest bony fish. It is also called the moonfish because of its round, flat body. The largest one ever recorded measured 10.2 ft. (3.1m) in length and 14 ft. (4.26m) in height from fin tip to fin tip. These bulky fish do not need to swim fast to catch their food, which is mainly jellyfish, as it drifts slowly through the water. A female sunfish can lay up to 300 million tiny eggs at one time. When the young hatch, they are smaller than a pea.

Water difference

Freshwater is less dense than saltwater, so it provides a little less support for the bodies of its inhabitants. It could be partly for this reason that fish living in rivers and freshwater lakes tend to be smaller than the creatures that swim in the sea. Other reasons for the size difference could be that there is less food and space available in many freshwater habitats than in the sea. Some giants, such as sturgeon and salmon, live and feed in saltwater but swim hundreds of miles upriver to lay their eggs.

River giants

The largest fish to spend its whole life in freshwater is the Mekong giant catfish, or pla buek. This rare fish can weigh up to 663 lbs. (300kg) and grow as long as 10 ft. (3m). It is threatened by heavy boat traffic, extensive overfishing, and the destruction of its breeding grounds in the Mekong river, which runs through Southeast Asia. Other giant catfish include the European, or wels, catfish, which once reached enormous lengths of more than 14 ft. (4.5m) and weights of more than 663 lbs. (300kg). Today the largest of these fish reach lengths of only 6.5 ft. (2m) and weights of 200 lbs. (90kg).

Super-sized squid

Squid range in size from tiny creatures that are as long as a thumbnail, to the 52-ft. (16-m)-long giant squid, to the colossal squid. If recent estimates are correct, it is feasible that the monstrous colossal squid could grow to almost twice the length of a giant squid.

Body beautiful

Squid are related to octopuses and cuttlefish. They have long, streamlined bodies, large heads, well-developed eyes, and poisonous, beaklike mouths ringed by ten long arms called tentacles. Two of the tentacles are much longer than the others and have suckers—or sometimes sharp claws— on the ends. The squid use these extra-long tentacles to grab prey. The body of most species is strengthened by a horny internal shell, called a gladius, which is shaped like a feather.

▲ Scientists gather a lot of information about the giant squid by using the specimens washed up on beaches. It is hard to gain an insight into their behavior since they have never been observed in their natural environment. Researchers are eager to film the giant squid and send cameras into the abyss on deep-diving submersibles or sperm whales in order to try to catch this squid sensation.

▶ Scientists estimate that a fully grown colossal squid could have a mantle (body) length of 13 ft. (4m). If the body grows in the same proportion as a giant squid, it could have tentacles reaching 82–98 ft. (25–30m) — that is almost the length of a tennis court!

giant squid   colossal squid

Colossal squid

In 2003 fishermen in the icy Ross Sea of Antarctica became the first people ever to see a colossal squid alive. It was feeding on a fish caught on their fishing lines, which were floating on the surface. Scientists estimate that this squid, which had a mantle length of 8.2 ft. (2.5m), was around half of its full size, so it could have grown much bigger than a giant squid. The colossal squid has a huge beak and unique rotating hooks on the clubs on the ends of its tentacles—not something you would want to bump into when you go for a swim in the ocean.

▼ A scientist examines the eye of a juvenile colossal squid caught in April 2003. Research to date suggests that the giant squid has the largest eyes of any living creature —they can grow to the size of a dinner plate. No one knows the eye size of a fully grown colossal squid, but it is sure to be immense.

Mysterious and huge

At least ten species of large squid, more than 6 ft. (2m) long, patrol the world's oceans, but as far as we know, none comes close in size to the colossal squid or the giant squid. These two mammoth creatures live deep down in the black depths of the oceans, and very little is known about their mysterious lives. No one has ever seen one in its natural habitat. We can piece together information about them only from eyewitness accounts of enormous squid seen from ships or from tentacles or bodies brought up to the surface in fishnets or washed up on the shore. Sperm whales hunt these great squid and have sometimes been found with huge tentacles in their stomachs and sucker-shaped scars on their skin. Some scientists believe that the whales injure or even kill these super-sized squid with a focused beam of sound.

◄ The Japanese spider crab is named after its long legs that look like a spider's legs. It lives in water as deep as 984 ft. (300m) in the Pacific Ocean off the coast of Japan. It moves slowly over the ocean floor on its spindly legs, scavenging for animal remains or feeding on live mollusks, crustaceans, and worms.

Sea monsters

Real sea monsters are much more extraordinary than those you read about in stories or legends. The ones you see on these two pages are all invertebrates—animals without internal bony skeletons—that can grow very large in the ocean with the support of the saltwater. It is unlikely that we know of every giant lurking in the myterious depths—these discoveries are still waiting to be made.

Mammoth mollusks

Several invertebrate giants, such as the giant octopus and giant clam, belong to a group of animals called mollusks, many of which have soft bodies with a hard casing for support and protection. The super-sized squid (see pages 54–55) and the giant octopus are both the biggest mollusks and the largest and smartest invertebrates. Octopuses are thought to be as intelligent as a pet cat! They have no shells, so they are very flexible in the water and are fast-swimming hunters with eight arms covered in suckers for swimming, gripping prey, and fighting.

Super stinger

The tentacles of the world's largest jellyfish, the Arctic lion's mane jellyfish, are armed with poisonous stingers instead of suckers. When prey (such as small fish, plankton, or even other jellyfish) swim into its long, trailing tentacles, they are injected with a paralyzing poison—called venom. This stops them from escaping while the jellyfish eats them.

Jellyfish were one of the first animals to live on Earth, and they have been swimming through the world's oceans for more than 600 million years. Today there are at least 200 different types of jellyfish, ranging from minis the size of a fingernail to jumbo jellies such as the lion's mane.

spider crab   giant octopus   lion's mane jellyfish

◄ The world's largest octopus is the shy Pacific giant octopus, which has an arm span of 8–13 ft. (2.5–4m)—the record is 31.5 ft./9.6m. Females have 280 suckers on each of their eight arms, making an extraordinary 2,240 suckers in total! To protect its soft body the giant octopus lives in rocky dens, reaching out with its long arms to grab crabs, smaller octopuses, and shellfish.

▲ The incredibly long, delicate tentacles of a lion's mane jellyfish trail out behind its body for up to 98 ft. (30m). With their tentacles fully extended, three of these huge jellyfish would stretch the length of a soccer field! At up to 7.5 ft. (2.28m) wide, the body of the lion's mane is much smaller than the tentacles but is still longer than the height of an adult human.

Longest legs

Crabs have also existed for a long time. Their basic body structure has stayed much the same for more than 200 million years. The largest crab alive today is the Japanese spider crab, which has a leg span of more than 13 ft. (4m)—that is almost the length of a small bus. Like all crabs, it has ten legs, not eight legs like spiders.

Crabs belong to a group of animals called crustaceans, whose bodies are protected and supported by hard, crustlike coverings. In order to get bigger, they have to grow new, larger body casings and shed, or molt, their old ones. Like Goliath tarantulas (see pages 22–23), crabs continue to molt as adults, which allows them to grow throughout their lives and to reach larger sizes. However, they cannot grow too big because their body casings would become so thick and heavy that the giants would not be able to move. It would also be difficult for a very large crab to stop its body from collapsing when it molted.

SUMMARY OF CHAPTER 3: GIANTS OF THE WATER

basking shark

your body feel lighter when you swim in a swimming pool or in the ocean.) If these huge sea monsters leave the water, they cannot support the weight of their heavy bodies, which slowly collapse.

Food for giants

The mightiest water giants feed on the smallest water creatures—the plankton that drifts close to the ocean's surface. Plankton is often called the "grass of the water" because it is the start of most ocean food chains, like grass is on land. There is an incredible amount of plankton floating in the sea, and it is rich in energy, allowing animals, such as baleen whales, to reach immense sizes.

Special support

The biggest creatures alive today, such as the blue whale, the whale shark, and the giant squid, all live in the vast spaces of the world's oceans. There the water pushes up against their bodies from below, supporting their massive weights. (You may have noticed how the water makes

Big mates, long lives

Large sizes may help both male and female sea giants survive and have larger offspring. Bigger male monsters win battles with other males for females, while enormous females have more energy reserves to feed and to care for their young. With fast or continuous growth and long life spans, the young can reach extraordinary sizes.

Go further . . .

For more information on the ocean sunfish visit: www.oceansunfish.org

Find out about the giant squid: www.giantsquid.org

Read about whales: www.enchanted learning.com/subjects/whales

For information about sharks and rays visit: www.sharktrust.org

Creatures of the Deep by Erich Hoyt (Firefly Books, 2001)

Giant Squid: Monsters of the Deep by Eulalia Garcia (Gareth Stevens, 1997)

Whales by Phil Clapham (Colin Baxter Photography, 1997)

Conservationist
Works to preserve wildlife habitats, save rare species, and find ways for people and animals to live together.

Ichthyologist
A biologist who chooses to concentrate on the study of fish.

Marine biologist
Studies sea creatures and how they live in the ocean environment.

Marine mammal scientist
A variety of careers is available such as: educator, researcher, animal trainer, field biologist, filmmaker.

Oceanographer
Studies the oceans.

Watch whale sharks and manta rays swimming past the biggest panoramic window in the world at:
Ocean Expo Park
Ishikawa 424 Motobu-cho
Okinawa 905-0206
Japan
Phone: 81 (0) 980 48 2741
www.ocean-park.go.jp

Experience the wonders of the underwater world at:
Sea World Orlando
7007 Sea World Drive
Orlando, FL 32821
Phone: (800) 327-2424
www.seaworld.com

Glossary

abdomen
The lower or rear part of an animal's body, which contains its digestive, reproductive, and waste disposal (excretory) systems.

abyss
The vast and inky black depths of the oceans.

amphibian
A cold-blooded animal with a backbone, such as a frog or a salamander, that lives on land and in water. Amphibians depend on water for breeding and do not have scaly skin.

antlers
The branching, bony structures growing from the top of a deer's head. Except for reindeer, only male deer have antlers.

Arctic
The region around the North Pole consisting of the Arctic Ocean and the tundra.

bacterium (plural: bacteria)
A simple, one-celled, microscopic life-form.

baleen
A tough, horny substance that forms fringed plates that hang from the top jaws of baleen whales, such as blue, fin, and sei whales, and are used to filter food from seawater.

blubber
A thick layer of fat between the skin and muscles of sea creatures such as whales, seals, and polar bears. It helps them stay warm and acts as a food reserve.

breeding season
The time of year when animals find mates and have young.

camouflage
Colors or markings that allow an animal to blend into its surroundings to avoid being seen.

carnivore
An animal that eats meat.

cold-blooded
An animal whose body temperature is the same as that of its surroundings.

constricting snake
A snake that coils its body around its prey. The prey, unable to breathe, dies of suffocation.

crustacean
An animal without a backbone that lives mainly in water and has a tough, chalky body case, jointed legs, and two pairs of antennae.

dentin
A hard substance that makes up the main part of the teeth of animals with backbones.

digestive system
The tubes and organs where food is broken down so it can be absorbed into the body.

exoskeleton
A hard shell or body casing that protects and supports the body. Many invertebrates (such as insects, spiders, clams, and crabs) and a few vertebrates (such as turtles and seahorses) have exoskeletons.

anaconda
constricting
a caiman

male Queen Alexandra's birdwing butterfly

ice age
Period of cold when ice covers most of Earth's surface. There have been several ice ages; the last one ended around 10,000 years ago.

ichthyosaur
An extinct reptile that looked like a dolphin and lived in the sea at the time of the dinosaurs.

insect
A small animal without a backbone that has three parts to its body and six legs. Most insects have wings and can fly.

insulation
Something that slows down the loss of heat such as fur, feathers, or blubber.

invertebrate
An animal with no backbone.

ivory
A type of dentin that makes up the tusks of animals such as elephants and walrus.

keratin
A horny material that makes up horns, hair, nails, fur, hooves, birds' bills, and reptiles' scales.

krill
Tiny crustaceans that swim in large schools on the surface of the sea.

life processes
The body processes common to all living creatures such as moving, feeding, breathing, excreting, growing, and reproducing.

mammal
A warm-blooded animal with fur or hair and a backbone. Mammals breathe air and feed their young on mother's milk.

maneuverable
Able to move quickly and with flexibility.

extinction
When a whole species of living things dies out and disappears forever.

fossils
Remains of living things preserved in rocks.

gills
The part of the body used by some water animals to take in oxygen from the water.

gladius
A stiff structure that supports a squid's body and forms a surface for muscle attachment.

habitat
The area in which an animal lives.

herbivore
An animal that eats only plants.

hibernation
A period of deep sleep that helps certain animals survive the winter when food is scarce.

mantle
A fold of skin covering the body of mollusks.

marrow
A soft, jellylike substance, rich in nutrients, that fills many bones.

migration
The annual journey made by some animals to find good weather, food, or a place to breed.

molar
A wide tooth at the back of a mammal's jaw with ridges for grinding and crushing up food.

mollusk
A soft-bodied animal without a backbone, whose body is often protected by a hard shell.

molting
The process of shedding an outer body layer such as fur, feathers, or skin. Animals with exoskeletons have to molt in order to grow bigger since their exoskeletons do not grow as fast as their bodies.

periscope
An instrument made with mirrors and a long tube to see things that are otherwise out of sight.

pinniped
A group of sea mammals that includes seals, walrus, and sea lions.

plankton
Microscopic plants and animals that drift close to the surface of oceans and lakes.

predator
An animal that hunts and kills animals (prey) for food.

prey
An animal that is hunted and eaten by other animals (predators).

protein
The chemical substances made by each cell in a living thing. They are needed as a building material or to control the chemical processes in cells.

pupa (plural: pupae)
The resting stage in the life cycle of certain

insects, during which time the body parts of the adult are built up inside a protective case.

rain forest
A dense, equatorial forest that is hot and wet all year long.

ratites
A group of flightless birds that have breastbones without a keel (a narrow ridge on the breastbones of flying birds for muscle attachment) and fluffy feathers with no barbs.

reptile
A cold-blooded animal with a backbone and scaly skin. Reptiles reproduce on land, mostly by laying eggs. The main reptile groups today are: snakes and lizards; tortoises and turtles; crocodiles and alligators.

scavenger
An animal that feeds mostly on animal remains.

sirenians
A group of sea mammals with smooth, hairless bodies and paddlelike front limbs. It includes three species of manatees and one species of dugong (sea cow).

skull crest
A bony structure sticking out of the top of the head. In pterosaurs it was probably used for balance or display.

species
A particular type of living thing that can mate with others of its kind to produce young.

streamlined
A slim shape that allows air or water to flow around the animal, enabling it to move fast.

submersible
A small submarine used for working deep in the sea.

talons
The sharp, curved claws used by birds of prey to kill their victims.

tentacle
A long, flexible, armlike structure close to an animal's mouth, used for catching food and also sometimes for moving.

trachea (plural: tracheae)
The tube through which air flows into the bodies of invertebrates. In vertebrates the trachea, or windpipe, is the airway leading from the throat to the lungs.

tropical areas
Parts of the world close to the equator where it is usually hot all the time.

tundra
Frozen lands around the polar regions where it is too cold for trees to grow.

tusk
A long, pointed tooth that sticks out of the mouths of animals such as walrus and elephants.

valve
A structure that controls the flow of blood so it moves in one direction and not backward.

venom
A poisonous fluid in the bite or sting of animals such as snakes and jellyfish.

vertebra (plural: vertebrae)
One of the bones that link together in a flexible chain to form the backbone of vertebrate animals.

vertebrate
An animal with a backbone, or spine.

warm-blooded
Being able to keep the body at the same warm temperature all the time. Only birds and mammals are warm-blooded.

a walrus (right) and a California sea lion (left) playing together

Index

Acknowledgments

The publisher would like to thank the following for permission to reproduce their material. Every care has been taken to trace copyright holders. However, if there have been unintentional omissions or failure to trace copyright holders, we apologize and will, if informed, endeavor to make corrections in any future edition.

Key: *b* = bottom, *c* = center, *l* = left, *r* = right, *t* = top

Front cover (*left to right*) Brandon Cole/Nature Picture Library, Frank Lane Picture Agency/© Minden Pictures, Steve Bloom; 1 Roland Seitre/Still Pictures; 2–3 National Geographic Image Collection/Michael Nichols; 4 Silvestris Fotoservice/NHPA; 7 Frank Lane Picture Agency/© Minden Pictures; 8*tl* © John Sibbick; 8–9*c* © John Sibbick ; 10*bl* M. & C. Denis-Huot/Still Pictures; 10–11*c* © Martyn Colbeck/Oxford Scientific Films; 11*tr* © Martyn Colbeck/Oxford Scientific Films; 12 Joel Sartore/National Geographic; 13 © Adrian Warren/Ardea.com; 14*bl* Whittaker/Frank Lane Picture Agency; 14*cl* and 15*bc* Mark Philips/Science Photo Library; 15*tr* © Nigel Dennis/NHPA; 15*br* Bettman/Corbis; 16*tl* © Nik Wheeler/Corbis; 16–17*c* Roland Seitre/Oxford Scientific Films; 17*tr* Jurgen Freund/Nature Picture Library; 18*tr* © Gus Christie/Wild Images/RSPCA Photolibrary; 18–19*c* © Albert Visage/Frank Lane Picture Agency; 20*tl* © Nick Gordon/ARDEA; 20*bl* Natural History Museum, London; 20–21*c* © The Natural History Museum, London; 21*br* Mark Moffet/Minden Pictures; 22*tl* © Tim Martin/Wild Images/RSPCA Photolibrary; 22–23*c* Oxford Scientific Films; 23*tr* ANT/NHPA Limited; 24*tl* Martin Harvey/NHPA; 24–25*c* Medford Taylor/National Geographic Image Collection; 25*tl* © Chris Hellier/Corbis; 25*tr* George Bernard/Science Photo Library; 26*tl* Mark Philips/Science Photo Library; 27 © Gerard Lacz/Frank Lane Picture Agency; 28–29 © John Sibbick; 30*bl* Ben Osborne/Nature Picture Library; 30*tr* Mary Evans Picture Library; 31*tr* © Wolfgang Kaehler/Corbis; 31*br* Mark Bristow; 32*bl* James Carmichael/NHPA Limited; 32–33 M. Watson/Ardea.com; 33*tc* Edward Julius Detmold, British Library, London, U.K./Bridgeman Art Library; 34–35*b* Dietmar Nill/Nature Picture Library, *c* Frank Lane Picture Agency/© Minden Pictures; 35*tr* Stephen Dalton/NHPA Limited; 36*cl* © Premaphotos; 36–37*c* Oxford Scientific Films; 37*br* Oxford Scientific Films; 38 J. & A. Scott/NHPA Limited; 39 Jurgen Freund/Nature Picture Library; 40–41 © John Sibbick; 42*bl* © Doc White/Seapics.com; 42–43*c* C. Neil Lucas/Nature Picture Library; 43*t* © Flip Nicklin/Minden Pictures; 44*tl* Brandon Cole/Nature Picture Library; 44–45*c* Fred Bruemmer/Still Pictures; 45*b* Brian Hawkes/NHPA Limited; 46 ANT/NHPA Limited; 47 J. & A. Scott/NHPA Limited; 48*tl* Clem Haagner/Ardea.com; 48*b* Ken Lucas/Ardea.com; 48–49*c* Daniel Heuclin/NHPA Limited; 49*tr* Staffan Widstrand/Nature Picture Library; 50*bl* Kev Deacon/Ardea.com; 50–51*c* Valerie Taylor/Ardea.com; 51*tr* © Douglas P. Wilson, Frank Lane Picture Agency/Corbis; 52*tl* © Flip Nicklin/Minden Pictures; 52*b* Ron Giling/Still Pictures; 53 © Richard Herrman/Seapics.com; 54*tl* Conrad Maufe/Nature Picture Library; 54–55*c* © Jurgen Ziewe; 55*br* © New Zealand Herald; 56*tl* Pat Morris/Ardea.com; 56–57*c* Jeff Rotman/Nature Picture Library; 57*tr* © Stuart Westmorland/Corbis; 58 Alan James/Nature Picture Library; 59 © Martin Wendler/NHPA Limited; 60 © Daniel Heuclin/NHPA Limited; 61 Joseph H. Bailey/National Geographic Image Collection; 64 Anup Shah/Nature Picture Library.

The publisher would like to thank John Sibbick for his excellent illustrations, David Burnie for his expert assistance, and Peter Denton of the WWF for his patience and efficiency.

The author wishes to thank Vicky Weber for her enthusiasm and support throughout this challenging project.